Psychic: F [illegible] t for

A Clear and Concise Guide on How to Allow and Naturally Develop Your Intuition and Psychic Abilities

by Natalie Nolan

Table of Contents

Introduction
5

What It Means to Be Psychic
8

The Different Types of Psychic Ability
13

Science Supporting Psychic Phenomenon
16

Modern Examples of Psychic Ability
21

Clairaudience:Working with Clear-Hearing
26

Meditation: The Main Tool for Psychic Ability
29
Discerning Ear Exercise
Hear the World Around You
Meditating on a Sound

Clairvoyance: Clear Seeing Abilities
34
Improving Your Physical Well-Being
Tapping into Your Intuition
Learning to Trust Exercise
Working with the Symbolic Mind
Using Zener Cards
Using Dreamwork to Improve Clairvoyance

Clairsentience & Claircognizance
43
Working with a Partner
Working with the Crown Chakra Exercise
Using Affirmations to Hone Your Abilities
Speak to the Divine
White Light Exercise

Clairolfactory & Clairgustance
54
Sweet & Sour Exercise
Improving Awareness to Heighten Senses

Psychometry
59
Opening Your Third Eye

Summary
61

Citations
63

Introduction

If you have chosen this body of work to read, you may or may not believe in psychic abilities, but you are demonstrating a serious interest in the subject. That's okay and as the author of this body of work, I encourage your skepticism. I do not want you to take the information I share with you here without encouraging you to use critical thought and for you to come up with your own conclusions and understandings about the subject matter. In fact, this body of work is not here to convince you, the reader, or anyone that psychic abilities are real, as it is up to everyone to decide if they want to openly accept such abilities as valid and legitimate. Instead, I offer this body of work as an explanation of the various subjects in which you now hold interest. It pleases me to offer some examples of real life experiences as well as early scientific evidence of the legitimacy of psychic abilities in all of us.

I encourage you to examine each chapter, familiarize yourself with the jargon and lingo associated with some of the more complex subjects, and to try some of the exercises in this book if you should decide you want to pursue your own abilities and strengthen them over the course of time. Now, if you are picking up this book in hopes of becoming an expert in some quick parlor tricks or you think you can become an expert in a few skills for the purposes of impressing others, this book really is not for you. The information contained within this book is for the skeptical or open minded reader willing to take the exploration of psychic abilities and information on how they work with an intense level of seriousness. Even in being skeptical it is still possible to approach the subject matter with respect which is what I recommend for every reader.

Now, at the offset, let us eradicate the common association with psychic abilities with Satan worship, the devil, evil, or any of the latter. The first thing everyone must embrace is just because something is strange to us or if we do not fully understand something, this does not make it a source of evil. In fact, there is nothing evil about one's psychic abilities and the only time such abilities might prove a bad thing is when a person chooses to harness them for the wrong reasons or to abuse the ability or to misuse their innate skills. Thus, it is not the abilities that one learns about or gains some control over that are the source of evil, rather, the person who chooses to behave in unethical ways that prove a bigger problem. If you want to awaken your own psychic talents, it might be a good time to explore and consider the reasons why you want to tap into your talents at this time in your life. Do you want to expand your knowledge, learn more about the world we live in, and use your abilities for the good of yourself and others, or are you considering exploiting your talents somehow? Taking up the art of awakening and strengthening psychic abilities is something you should do with pure intentions as exploitation will only end in trouble in the long run, and, in fact, may serve as a means of disconnecting you from your psychic talents all together.

Ultimately, if you have picked this body of work to explore the concept of psychic phenomena, the subject has piqued your interests. Maybe you just read a book where the main character had psychic abilities or you watched a film where someone was using psychic talents. Or, you suspect someone you know has such an ability or maybe you are even tuning into your own psychic resources. If that is the case, then congratulations on your awakening. You will find some amazing discoveries as your psychic abilities begin to reemerge or finally completely emerge from their seeming slumber! I hope this body of work can help serve as an introduction to your own abilities and what you can do with them: Thus, may this work serve as a beacon of light to reveal the path to greater wisdom, knowledge, and psychic understandings!

What It Means to Be Psychic

So, what is the meaning of psychic or being a psychic? Per the Etymology Dictionary Online, the term psychic has some fascinating etymological roots. By the early 1640s the term was used in literature as "physical," but later, in the early 1870s, it was used as a reference to something associated with the human soul. The root of the word comes from the ancient Greek psykhikos, meaning the mind, spirit, or soul, and from psyche, meaning "life or soul." The first time the term was associated with the ability to have consciousness of things without explanation was in 1871 when the term came to represent what we now understand to be psychic gifts. Today, the term psychic refers to a set of abilities that can be used to gain knowledge without the need for conscious reasoning, assumptions, or deductions. When using psychic abilities, a person knows something intuitively through a form of "unconscious cognition, instinctive understanding, or an inner sensing/knowing. In 1870, the same term is used to describe a person that relies on such abilities, in other words, a psychic was, at that time, equivalent to a medium.

Today the terms psychic and medium are interchangeable; however, there can be some subtle differences between the two: This most certainly is true when considering things like spirit connection. A medium is someone who can connect with spirit and who is likely to have awakened psychic abilities, whereas a psychic gains information through the reception of vibrational energies associated with people, events, or even an object. At the same time, when it comes to medium-like skills, the psychic might not have mastered a full understanding or method for making connection with Spirit or the spirit world. When a psychic picks up on these vibrational energies, it is not through the act of conscious reasoning: Some might call this intuition, inner sensing, unconscious cognition, or "knowing without knowing" (the source from which gives the knowledge is unknown to the receiver of the information).

Some people call this sixth-sense a special gift and feel only a select few can tap into such abilities. However, there are those that assert that these gifts are available to us all if we are willing to nurture them and hone them. The difficulties often arise in what we are taught as children that only science is correct and that which is not visible or that falls under the category of supernatural/paranormal is not reality-based. Yet, it's also possible to argue that just because you cannot see something doesn't mean it doesn't exist, and just because you may not have nurtured the ability, perhaps due to your disbelief in such experiences, doesn't mean you do not have them or cannot hone them.

When examining any material on psychic abilities it really is only fair if we look at the subject from all angles, including what the majority say. Thus, we must consider the disbelief in psychic abilities. The other side of accepting the existence and validity of psychic experiences is embracing the understanding of those who are skeptical.

Of course, skeptics believe that psychic experiences have a logical or simple explanation, citing Occam's razor as the best means for determining the validity of any claim of having a psychic experience. Occam's Razor (or Ockham's Razor), also known as the "Law of Parsimony," was established by the Franciscan friar William Ockham. William was born in 1287 C.E. and was a theologian as well as a scholar. Ockham's Razor is a philosophical concept suggesting when comparing two or more conditions where assumptions are made about a said condition/situation/event, the explanation presenting with the fewest hypotheses or conjectures is most likely the correct answer. Thus, in the final analysis, the conclusion is that there must be a far simpler explanation for having psychic experiences like de ja vu where you've seen something before and only later recall it and think it is a psychic experience. Or being exposed to data that becomes a particle of memory until you retrieve it in the future: This small memory, having no importance when you encountered the action or situation, gains significance only when you apply it by pulling it up and suggesting you've seen it before or that it has some meaning to a current situation. Yes, many people will claim it is all in the head and that the way we perceive the world and make assumptions explain away the validity of psychic phenomenon.

Interestingly, the word skepticism is really taken as a total disbelief in psychic phenomenon when the very definition of the word signifies one who has a questioning or doubting attitude about something. If we next consider the word doubt and its meaning, it suggests "uncertainty" versus the strange certainly in disbelief the use of the work skeptic seems to convey. Essentially, to say "I am a skeptic," equals in the mind of the speaker, "I am a disbeliever because I am sensible and rational," whereas the real meaning of the word should have the person thinking "I am not sure if psychic abilities are real or not, but I am open to finding out more information."

Thankfully, this book is not written in an effort to convince the non-believer in such phenomenon. In fact, while a healthy dose of skepticism is always recommended as it will allow you to consider things with a critical eye, it is this same skepticism when taken to the extreme and is misinterpreted in meaning that closes the doors on the possibilities of identifying or appreciating natural or innate psychic talents. A fixed mind is closed, and this body of work is not intending to pry at those metaphorically closed doors. Hopefully, when viewing this book and its material with an open eye, you will have enough information to sway you of the reality of psychic abilities and how they can serve you in your life or serve to help others when you tap into your natural abilities.

Exploring the Different Types of Psychic Ability

When you first start out with an interest in psychic phenomena, you have either heard of someone having such experiences or you might think you have had some of your own. There are many ways to receive psychic messages and imagery, and it is true that we often receive such messages and do not even realize it is. For example, some of the simplest messages we receive are not really messages at all, but rather markers or indicators showing we have psychic potential.

Have you ever been sitting around doing whatever it is you are doing during the day and then suddenly someone you have not thought of in a long time pops up in your mind? Maybe you are just thinking about this person and you see them in your mind's eye, and the next thing you know your doorbell rings, and there they are standing in front of you after a number of years apart, or your phone rings and it's their voice greeting you on the other end of the line. Maybe you've been driving your car down the road when suddenly a song you haven't heard for years pops up in your mind and then 2 minutes later it starts to play on the radio. Maybe you had a dream about something that happens to you at work, and then you head for work and the very dream you have comes back perfectly thereby giving you the eeriest sense of *de ja vu* you've ever experienced. Or maybe you've smelled something, like the scent of a cigar when no one is around and it immediately conjures up images of your cigar smoking grandfather: Bear in mind that the sensory experiences of smell and memory are grossly interlinked.

All of the above-mentioned scenarios are the ways in which some psychic experiences present themselves. You might hear a voice telling you information that is true, valid, and yet, you have no way of knowing the actual origin of such information. You might see something in your mind's eye as it plays out like it's on a movie screen in your mind. You might feel strange sensations or pick up on emotional responses of another.

You might smell something or even taste something without having outside physical stimuli responsible for the sensations. Perhaps you suddenly hear something with your inner ears providing you with much needed guidance.

Dreaming is another means of receiving psychic information, and you might even find you can pick up on the thoughts of another without them speaking to you and vice versa. The pathways in which psychic experiences occur are myriad and worthy of much exploration.

The Science Supporting Psychic Phenomenon

Nikola Telsa, an electrical engineer and genius in his own time, once suggested that when science begins the exploration of the non-physical phenomena, only then will it make the speediest progress in terms of discovery. He also argued that the universe's true nature was one of vibration, frequency, and energy: It is this energy and vibrations that a psychic senses tune into; though unseen, it is possible to tap into these energies using our innate, psychic abilities. These energies can be detected through different abilities, each running in a similar but very different manner. You may have one, more, or all of the abilities herein mentioned. Some may be immediately recognizable and others might have yet been recognized or triggered/awakened. You will likely find, however, that you have at one least ability that seems stronger than the rest and this is your dominant ability: You might want to put special focus on this one ability as you proceed to work with your psychic senses and training them accordingly.

In a write-up appearing in *National Geographic* by Susan Brink entitled *"ESP is Put to the Test*

– *Can You Foretell the Result?"* the author explores some of the tests conducted throughout the history of research pertaining to extra sensory perception. One of the earliest studies conducted by an academic is the one undertaken at Duke University by Joseph Bank Rhine in the early 1930s with findings that ended up in the *Boston Society of Psychic Research* publication. Responsible for what we now know as Zener

cards which are cards with five different symbols on them, including a star, square, wavy lines like water, a circle, and an equal-armed cross, each deck had a total of 25 cards in them. These cards were presented to subjects to see if they could accurately predict the symbol that might come up on the card that they would see next. In a single experiment where 2400 "guesses" were made by participating subjects, some 489 predictions were true, whereas five correct answers out of the 25 would give a result that is greater than chance. The findings of the study produced and outcome that was greater than twice the number of findings one would need to attribute it to chance alone. Skeptics will assert that the testing was poorly conducted or that the participants likely cheated during the test, and those a bit more open minded suggest the likelihood of such findings is a ridiculously high probability or there is something else that is not understood happening.

According to a write-up appearing in the Cornell Chronicle by George Lowery, Dr. Daryl Bem has conducted some studies indicating that humans, indeed, demonstrate some psychic abilities. Over the course of eight years and work with over 1,000 participants, Dr. Bem has revealed that humans do have a mild ability to "anticipate the future." Bem, of course, is talking about precognition, or presentiment if you want to talk about in nice, acceptable, scientific terms, a concept that continues to fascinate him because he knows it is not some magical or whimsical phenomenon.

Daryl Bem is a Professor of Psychology Emeritus and his findings were published in the *American Psychological Associations Journal of Personality and Social Psychology*. Now before being a student of psychology, Dr. Bem also took up a study of physics. He eventually became interested in the "unexplained processes of energy or data transfer or psi phenomena" when he was asked to examine the works of another psi researcher in an effort to find mistakes in the research ... in other words, so he could debunk it and have it written off as nonsense. Guess what, he couldn't find any mistakes in the research done by the fellow researcher. His pioneering work and findings has resulted in studies indicating that we have physiological responses to things we are about to be exposed to before the exposure even occurs: In other words, we have a heightened detection of something underway before it occurs and our body begins to respond to that heightened awareness even if we don't know what it is that is coming up for us in the near future. Of course, there are those who continue to disbelieve the assertions set for in Dr. Bem's work and they call it nothing but nonsense, while others are working hard to replicate the findings.

First, let us do away with the notion that we fully understand the very basics of physical sensory information and how we receive it. In fact, we know too little. Yes, we are aware of our eyes, ears, nose, mouth, as well as our sense of touch, and our brain and how it all interacts, but there is so much about the human body that is yet misunderstood. In *The Scientist* online, author Mary Beth Aberlin mentions some interesting things about sensory information in the human body in the article *"A Cornucopia of Sensory Perception,"* as the writing contains material that encourages us to forget what we think we know about human beings and the sensory systems:

> *"The human body also contains sensory receptors where you would never expect them. It seems fantastical to say that*

skin, kidneys, muscles, and even sperm can smell; that light-sensitive pigments in blood vessels can make those vessels relax; that taste receptors in our guts can go "yuck" to pathogens and bacteria."

The above passage alone makes clear that we have little understanding of all the physical sensory data we receive, and we should, therefore, make no assumptions about the sensory data we are receiving through alternative means. We shouldn't be so quick to write something off as non-existent simply because we cannot fully explain its origin or how it works. The jury is still out in the academic and scientific settings as far as whether psychic phenomena is real or bunk. It is up to us as individuals to decide what we believe is the truth of the matter. It is for these individuals this book is produced and will now delve into the unique abilities among us and how they might be improved upon or harnessed for greater use.

Modern-Day Examples of Psychic Experiences

Psychic experiences have been reported from people from all walks of life and this includes modern day celebrities. These reports are sometimes shared through media outlets and such incidents reveal uncanny, inexplicable occurrences believed to be real life psychic episodes. The modality in which a person experiences a psychic episode differs in each case, as is revealed in the stories shared below. The examples shared here first appeared in a report in The Epoch Times in an article entitled "**Celebrities Who Had Premonitions That Came True**."

Some psychic events demonstrate the long term and most remarkable human connection between two people who are long-time friends. For example, on June 20, 2011, actor and stuntman Ryan Dunn, 34, who one of MTV's stars of the hit show *Jackass*, died in a car crash after achieving a speed of 100 mph and crashed into a wooded embankment at exactly 12:30 pm, the vehicle caught fire and took the life of Dunn and his passenger Zach Heartwell. Dunn's closest friend since age 11, Bam Margera, reported losing control of himself in an unexplainable act of physical outrage, but states he wasn't mad at anyone at the time but was still feeling rage for what he thought was no reason at all. This incident occurred at the precise time the accident did, so much so he began smashing the windows of the rental van he was in at the time for what he says "was no reason at all."

Another well-known Irish celebrity, Liam Neeson, famed for his roles in movies like *Schindler's List* and *Taken*, was notified of his father's death in the most unusual way. When Liam was a young boy, his father once cared for birds, and when Liam had a small red bird enter his apartment, fly about, and then fly back outside through the window it had entered, the bird immediately conjured up images of his father when he was younger. Within the hour, Liam was notified of his father's passing, but even more uncanny is the fact that Liam's sister, who was in an entirely different location had a similar experience with a pigeon that appeared with a broken leg, triggering remembrances of her father. In an interview once Liam explained the legend of birds getting inside the home and their association, symbolically speaking, of birth or death. This incident might indeed be evidence of the psychic connection between the children and their father, but also of how animals can sometimes appear and bring with them messages from beyond. It definitely gives a whole new meaning to the notion of *"a little birdy told me."*

Sometimes, as is evidenced by the next account, psychic events can occur years before what is predicted happens. For example, the parents of Reeva Steenkamp reveal how she once drew a picture when she was a teen that seems to have an ominous meaning now, wherein she illustrated a person with a gun, an angel, and a long stairway leading up to the heavens. Reeva grew to be an adult and began dating Oscar Pistorius, the Olympian who ended up being on trial for killing her on February 14, 2013. She was shot to death because Pistorius allegedly believed she was an intruder in the home.

Regardless of the uncanniness of such occurrences, scientists have documented changes in the brain during psychic experiences. Appearing in an article on Dr. Oz, Dr. Amen, a psychiatrist and brain imaging specialist as well as the Founder of the Amen Clinic explains these changes that occur in the brain. In the *"Neuroscience of Psychic Experience,"* Amen explains how the brain behaves by demonstrating a decreased level of activity in the right temporal lobe function and how this activity looks a lot like the brain when a person is having a seizure. Amen also writes how psychic experiences tend to increase especially when a person has had a brain injury affecting the right brain hemisphere.

Jeffry Mishlove, Ph.D., is an author, psychologist, and the host of *New Thinking Allowed*. He conducted an interview with neuropsychiatrist Vernon Neppe who is also the head of the Pacific Neuropsychiatric Institute based in Seattle, Washington. The interview involved the discussion of how the brain works during psychic experiences. During the interview, Neppe discusses how people experience and feel psychic phenomena, but how there may be something more happening that occurs outside of the brain or even outside of the individual receiving the psychic information. Thus, it is possible that we are picking up information that occurs outside of our body, or, as some suspect, human consciousness itself is outside of the body, and we are detecting something that has an effect on our physical and paraphysical senses.

It is worthy of noting that there have indeed been instances where works of art and creative works have provided predictive in nature. Once such example is the novel: *Futility,* written in 1898 by Morgan Robertson. The novella told the fictional account of an ocean liner that had set sail in the North Atlantic. The boat strikes an iceberg and sinks. If this is already sounding familiar, it should, as it sounds exactly like the RMS Titanic that sunk into the icy waters of the North Atlantic 2 hours and 40 minutes after striking an iceberg. However, the RMS was a tragedy that occurred on April 14, 1912, some 14 years before the writing of *Futility*. What's even more disturbing is the similarities don't stop there. The name of the boat in the *Futility* ... The Titan, which seems perfectly fitting given the topic of discussion. The Titan and the Titanic both failed to have sufficient numbers of lifeboats for the passengers on board. The Titan is written as being 800 feet in length and the Titanic 882 feet. The Titan was moving at 25 knots, and the Titanic at 22.5 knots. Both vessels were said to be "unsinkable," both has triple screw propellers, both had limited lifeboats, both hit an iceberg on the starboard side of the vessel; both vessels sunk into the ocean on an April evening at 400 nautical miles from Terranova; both reported massive loss of life due to the tragedy. Indeed, the sinking of the Titanic is and will always be a massive tragedy. In fact, the only tragedy that could prove worse is if we were forewarned some 14 years prior to the incident that the tragedy would occur ... so the question is, were we warned ahead of time through the writing of *Futility*? The idea is certainly something amazing to consider.

Clairaudience: Working with Clear-Hearing Abilities

As per the New World Encyclopedia online, clairaudience is merely a word that literally means "clear hearing," and it is a form of hearing that occurs without the actual physical act of auditory trigger or response. The hearing occurs on a supernatural or "paranormal" level wherein the individual hears something but no physical or reasonable explanation can be cited as the source of that hearing. The individual might hear words or a sound of some kind that no one else hears, or the same thing might be heard by more than one individual but then does not show up on any recording equipment.

Some refer to clairaudience as the "inner mental form of listening or words being heard that are absent of any impressions on an auditory level." If it is a medium working with spirits, then the medium might feel he or she is in direct reception with the thoughts or feelings of an energetic being, one who has passed or is from the Spirit realm. It is imperative to note however that messages received through clairaudience differ significantly from a person who might have a mental illness of some kind associated with psychosis, a break from reality, or hearing voices. If you are hearing voices telling you to do something wrong or to harm yourself and others, it's time to put down this book and immediately head to the doctor for further assistance.

Now some who have had clairaudient experiences claim to hear a whisper or a clear statement in their mind by a voice that is outside of themselves. This voice seems to be right near the area of the ear when it is detected, but a bit closer to the temple and cheek than right at the location where one's ear is actually located. What is clear is that the voice, once detected, is one that the hearer might at first identify as stemming from one's own thoughts, but they are often supplied with information they would have no way of knowing and the questioning of how one might know such information triggers the recognition of the voice as being external to the self and not of one's own generated thoughts.

Two types of clairaudience exist, which are referred to as objective and subjective clairaudient experiences. The clairaudient experience that is objective is one experienced outside of yourself and/or where others experience the sound with you. The subjective clairaudient experience is only heard by your inner or paraphysical ears. Sometimes the sounds you are very clear and as if they are coming from someone in the same room or vicinity as you, or even right next to you. Other times, the sounds you pick up on may be faint, fuzzy, sound static-like, or as if they are coming from underwater. Other times the sounds you hear might be sing-songy, rhythmic or even dreamy. When your skill is just presenting itself, you might not receive full clairaudient messages, you will hear a few sounds, a word or two, or you may hear things but not be able to discern them very well. With practice and concentration, this can improve over time. Focusing in on the sounds you are hearing is key to improving clairaudient skills, again as it triggers to brain into knowing you are paying attention and interested in the information you are attempting to access.

Meditation: Your Main Tool for Psychic Ability

Meditation is one of the major tools people use to improve psychic abilities. To learn how to still the mind, to enter into quiet contemplation and to discipline the self has myriad health benefits. But meditation has also demonstrated an ability to increase one's ability to connect to the energy vibrations that otherwise trigger or incite psychic phenomena. Daily meditation, even if only performed five minutes a day, can help a person tune into their own thoughts and therefore more easily identify thoughts or ideas they are detecting from some outside source. When learning to meditate, you can clear your head and then more readily pick up on information that is beyond the physical self, including sensations, feelings, emotions, and visual as well as auditory information.

Some people struggle with meditation, finding it difficult to achieve a state of no-thought and quietness. To that end, one only need to sit quietly, to focus on the inhalation and exhalation of the breath, and to merely let thoughts flow and let them go. Over the course of time, you will gain greater control of your meditation practices so you can control what thoughts you allow to exist in the mind during your sessions. Simply sitting down to meditate each day also states an intent and allows the mind and body to know that you are making an effort to tune into your abilities. Becoming a creature of habit will make meditation practices much easier, and with a focus on intent in the early morning hours, you can then begin to plan how your day will play out before it plays out in real life. It is a good idea to document your experiences to see if your intentions are then reflected in reality.

By demonstrating that you can use intention to shape your experiences before they happen, you are demonstrating the ability to define your conscious experiences before they occur, likewise, psychic experiences are along the same lines and will notify you of potential experiences before they happen. Much like psychokinetic energy which allows a person to interact with the physical to make things move without touching them, you can use intent to predefine and arrange experiences beforehand and without interacting with anything physically to do so at the time when you are envisioning the intentions you want to manifest.

Be creative and visual: Using your imagination to visualize anything or to create a work of art of any kind, these things also increase your ability to see in your mind, the images you want to hold. Of course, the secondary benefit of creativity is that it allows you to connect to the universal source of all, and to go within. Working with art can be much like an act of meditation, especially if you lose yourself in the process, relax, and simply enjoy the creative session as you work.

Discerning Ear Exercise

If you have ever played a musical instrument in a group before, then this exercise should be easy for you. If not, you can still train yourself to do this exercise which involves learning to listen to a single instrument at a time while tuning out others. Choose any genre music you like, although classical music is the one that works best for this exercise as it helps relax the mind while you focus on the different instruments playing. While listening, tune into the first violin and only that instrument. Do this for a while and then shift to the second violin, viola, cello, or bass. You can tune into any instrument you want but do so for an extended period of time. This will help you developing your focus and intentional or discerning hearing abilities: By sharpening this skill, when a clairaudient experience occurs, you will be able to tune into the message better while tuning out all the other sounds around you that are invading your physical senses.

Hear the World Around You

It is a fact that if one of our physical senses becomes disabled or we end up losing that sense all together, then the remarkable human body allows our other senses to become stronger in an effort to make up the difference for the physical sense we lost. That being the case, if you want to hone your clairaudient paraphysical sense, you can start by closing your eyes or even blindfolding yourself. To take away sight lets you use your ears for greater focus. Now, sit quietly indoors or outdoors and just listen, really listen for the first time to your environment. Notice every sound, but particularly those you tune out every single day. When you are finished with this assessment write down what you can remember hearing. Do this daily so you can improve your ability to pick up on background noises and other sounds you might others dismiss during the course of a given day. Ultimately, this exercise helps hone in on what you want to hear with greater clarity.

Meditating on a Sound

A singing bowl is a good tool for this exercise, but if you do not have one, you can simply sit in meditation and imagine a sound. It might be the sound of a dog barking or a single musical note, it makes no difference. Just as long as you focus on imagining the sound as perfectly and as long as possible. Meditation gives you time to still the mind, and when concentrating on a sound you being to build your focusing abilities.

Clairvoyance: Working with Clear-Seeing Abilities

Clairvoyance is derived from the French and can be interpreted as clear seeing, but it's not with the physical eyes that one is seeing something. Rather, in the mind's eye or inside of one's head is where the vision takes place. Some psychics explain that they feel as if the vision is right on their forehead at the location of the third eye, while others report seeing something akin to a film running or projecting an image in their mind. These visions supply the recipient with information about people, places, and things, sometimes stemming from the past, but also sometimes stemming from the future as well.

Clairvoyance occurs in three different types of experience with the first being precognition, the second retrocognition, and the third being remote viewing. Precognition is seeing something happening before it occurs. Retrocognition is seeing something stemming from the past. Remote viewing is seeing something at a distant location in which the psychic has no way of knowing about otherwise.

Improving Your Physical Well-Being

With a focus on the body and diet, you can improve your physical well-being. Make sure you are getting adequate nutritional intake, and that you are exercising regularly. What does this have to do with paraphysical senses? When your body is healthy you can increase your vibrations and with an increased vibration you can pick up on things with greater ease psychically speaking.

Tapping into Your Intuition

For this exercise, you need to prepare yourself like you are going to meditate. The area needs to be quiet and free of distractions so make sure there is little noise in the background and that you won't be interrupted until you finish with this exercise. You will start by focusing on your breathing and bringing a deep breath in and exhaling very slowly. Inhale slowly, and then exhale once more. The aim is to achieve a relaxed state.

Now, focus on a problem you've been dealing with in your daily life; it can be any problem you want a solution too. Speak in your mind directly to your Higher Self or Guide and ask for assistance with the issue at hand. Concentrate on all aspects of the problem and what will you think might happen if the problem is not solved. If and when you receive guidance, do not doubt it. Thank the Higher Self or Guide for the assistance provided and trust it will come. Now let the problem dissolve out of your mind. If you don't get an immediate answer, repeat the exercise until you do. You may have to wait for your vibration to be just right to tune into the Higher Self. If you do get an answer, implement it immediately. Document the answers you receive and the results. Even if you don't think the solution has merit, implement it anyway. Remember that you need to trust the intuition you are tapping into at the time.

Learning to Trust Exercise

If new to receiving clairvoyant images, the recipient might see fuzzy or fragmented images or they might only see brief and fleeting sightings. It is therefore very easy to dismiss what one is receiving as imagination. Sometimes, instead of presenting the psychic with entire pictures and narratives, the psychic might only see symbols that will later have to be interpreted for meaning. ***The key to sharpening this skill is to pay attention to the messages you are receiving and to not dismiss them as a product of the imagination.*** Learning to trust your skills is one of the hardest things you'll ever do as a psychic, but the more you begin to trust, the more open you become to the messages you can then pick up in the future.

Often times, clairvoyant images come to you spontaneously, and for a fleeting moment you wonder where the images come from or what they mean; then your own thoughts come into play and immediately you begin to doubt the clairvoyant message you've sensed. Not only does this weaken the connection to whatever vibration you have picked up on, it has now left you not believing what at least one of your psychic senses are telling you. Here's what you need to do to stop doubting so much and to start giving your visions the serious consideration they deserve:

1. Instead of doubting, document what you see, reflect on it, and if you see symbols, interpret them and document your interpretations.

2. Draw what you see; it doesn't have to be a Picasso either, just make an attempt to draw what you see in your mind's eye as

best you can: This helps sharpen focus over the course of time, and also teaches you how to really look at a scene or scenario when it is part of a vision presented to you.

3. Practice focusing on a single image for as long as you can and then put the image away. After five minutes, bring up the image in your mind and look at with intense detail. Make it conjure up in your mind exactly the way you saw it in the physical: This makes use of your natural visualization skills and will sharpen your ability to see more clearly with your mind's eye. It will also help you look at all visions as if you are an artist assessing a work of art: Doing this improve small detail recall.

4. Document everything you can recall before a moment of doubt crawled into your mind and sabotaged the scene by reorienting you to the physical world around you instead of allowing you to maintain the psychic connection.

5. Consider the nature of your visions when they come to you: Are you looking at symbols or is the vision to be taken literally? Often times, the visions that make no sense whatsoever, as if you are

seeing something taken out of context, are symbolic.

6. Make sure you note successes and failures of when your visions appeared correct or provided you with foreknowledge about something. Make sure you track failures too, as this is important if you are going to trust yourself and your guides along the way.

Working with the Symbolic Mind

The mind, particularly the subconscious and the Higher Self will communicate through the use of symbols a lot. To put this into an exercise, all you need is a pencil and some paper. If you want colored pencils feel free to use them as colors have important symbolism too. Sit in a quiet area and ask of the Higher Self for some insight into your life or a situation you are dealing with at the time. Wait for a few minutes and see if any image comes to your mind. If not, repeat the process.

Eventually something will come to your mind that will serve as a symbol. Use the very first thing that comes to mind and do not doubt the image. Now sketch it. After sketching it discern what it means to you. Do not rush to a symbol dictionary first, instead rely on your own built in understanding of symbols. For example, if you see a bald eagle this might mean "freedom" to you. If you see a pink "rose" this might mean love. Decide what the symbol means and meditate on the meaning for greater understanding.

Using Zener Cards

Zener cards, as mentioned earlier, are an excellent tool you can use to sharpen your precognition and visual skills. Each card needs to be face down before it is presented. Write down what you predict each card is before you flip it over. You will want to work toward achieving a goal of getting the right answer greater than 50% of the time which is beyond mere chance. You can make your own set by including the following symbols on them:

You don't have to use a deck of cards physically either. You can also use cards online through any site offering free ESP testing and games.

Using Dreamwork to Improve Clairvoyance

Dreams are methods for you to tap into your subconscious or your higher self to learn more about yourself, but also the external world. It is not at all uncommon for people to have dreams that predict real life occurrences. Some of the most famous people in the world have had precognitive dreams. Take for example, Abraham Lincoln who foresaw others crying and mourning over the death of the president and whose somber dreams of boats riding off into the murky and foggy distance held an ominous omen for him most his adult life. Or consider the dreams Caesar's wife had of his eventual betrayal and murder, and even though forewarning him of what she had seen, she could not prevent the devastating event that took her husband's life. Alexander the Great had dreams showing him of daily life affairs and happenings.

For years, people have claimed to have dreams right before some natural disaster or some of the most devastating events in history. For example, there were some who were said to cancel their trip on the Titanic after having dreams of its destruction (a wise decision indeed), and others have laid claim to having dreams before airline crashes, shootings, and even the Roman Emperor Nero's mother had premonitions occur to her in dreams where she dreamt she would ultimately bear witness to the birth of monster. Story after story exists of those receiving communication from the spirit world and bring back important messages from beyond as well.

If you are looking to tap into your psychic abilities, particularly clairvoyance but also clairaudience too, these dreamtime presentations are not to be ignored. As you pay more attention to what your dreams are sending you in the way of visions, messages, and communications, you'll begin to have more dreams that do the same. The subconscious awakens to the attentiveness of the conscious mind and a deeper, more powerful connection is made. To record your dreams is the first step into, not just understanding them, but beginning to pick up on when a dream is premonitory or not. Ancient and modern oneiromanticists as well as psychologists from twentieth century like Sigmund Freud would first suggest looking to dream images and narratives for the double entendres and the punning that often appear there and that can be interpreted into messages for the dreamer.

An interpretation of the symbolism behind whatever images one sees is another measure for perhaps picking up on premonitory information.

Clairsentience & Claircognizance

Clairsentience refers to "clear-feeling," and is one of the most common psychic abilities people have but do little to acknowledge. With this ability, you can pick up on the atmosphere of a room or the emotions of another, whether living or whether those vibrations come from the past. If you've ever had a "vibe" about someone as being a good or bad person, this is your clairsentience ability revealing itself. With this ability, you can sense the feelings and emotions of spirits, people, and even animals as well as any kind of vibrations that might be in the immediate environment. Ever walk into a room where two people were arguing but you had no way of knowing that beforehand? Nevertheless, when you walk in the room the negative vibration practically smacks you in the face? That's clairsentience in action.

Sometimes what you can pick up on can be so emotionally overwhelming it may confuse you too; you can be in a perfectly good mood and the next thing you know you're depressed or even crying without knowing why. This comes from being a natural empath. Being in a public place or crowd can make an empath uncomfortable or downright upset depending on who they come in contact with and until they learn how to control when they are open to picking up vibrations and when they are closed they may avoid crowds altogether. Usually these same people care for others deeply and easily relate to them in some way because they can literally walk in their shoes, at least in an emotional sense. Of course, another clue that your clairsentience abilities are strong occurs when you see someone injured whether in person or on television or in the movies and you temporarily sense the pain in the same area of the body that the individual injured. There are several exercises you can do in order to improve your clairsentient abilities.

Working with a Partner

Ask a close friend or family member to help you with some of your psychic exercises. But, here is a word of warning, don't choose someone that doubts the possibility of psychic phenomenon or someone who will not take the effort just as seriously as you do. You want positive energies and vibrations surrounding every exercise you perform. Negative thought patterns can interrupt the flow of things and may even end up blocking your abilities to pick up on things. Besides, you don't want to be self-conscious as you work on perfecting your natural psychic abilities in front of a die-hard skeptic.

Have the individual bring several photographs of people they know but you do not know. Make sure it is no one you know even by word of mouth because you run in close circles. The more distant the individual is from you the better.

Take one photo at a time and work with it. Don't rush, and record the session so you can latter document your hits and misses. Have the person state the person's name in the photo and focus in on the person and the image. Say whatever comes to mind and do not try to logically consider what it is you are looking at when you look at the picture. If a nickname comes to you, say it. If you see this person in a scene like a clairvoyant experience, announce what you are seeing in your mind's eye. If you hear words, say them aloud and note the clairaudient experiences. If your High Self provides you with a message for this individual through claircognizant abilities, speak it aloud. If you feel things or sense emotions, announce the clairsentient experience and again, document it. When you feel you have finished, let the person go over everything you have said and suggested in order to see the level of accuracy you have.

A word of warning here: It is best to go through all the photos before checking for accuracy. If you only go through one photograph and then assess your findings for accuracy, if you are not very accurate with the first, doubt may taint the findings in the readings that follow. Do not allow the element of doubt to creep into the practice work as this can lead to nothing but inaccurate guesswork and frustration.

Claircognizance, meaning clear thought or clear knowing, is having access to information that you know is accurate or that proves accurate later on when you investigate, without having any psychical explanation as to why you would have such knowledge in the first place. With this kind of "knowing without knowing" you are absolute in terms of certainty in regards to its accuracy. You might convey concrete facts, but sometimes you simply might know the truth about something that you have no real way of knowing at all. When you put this talent to use, it is usually at random and it typically serves as an alert system: One that lets you know there is something not quite right or that something is about to go wrong. For example, imagine driving down the highway and then sensing that for whatever reason you should avoid your usual route. You do so, and then scold yourself for driving out of your way when you really didn't have too. Later, you discover a terrible accident on the road you would have taken had you not listened to your psychic guidance. Essentially, claircognizance is direct information received from your Higher self without the introduction of other paraphysical or physical senses.

When looking to improve claircognizance abilities, you are going to have to make sure your crown chakra is open so you can receive messages with ease. The crown chakra is located at the top of the head, hence why it is called the crown chakra.

You will become aware of what a claircognizant experience feels like when you get a gut feeling that something is right, true, or accurate and you have no doubt in your mind about the knowledge you have despite not being able to trace the knowledge to a physical origin, encounter, event, or source. The onset of a claircognizant experience is often rapid, spontaneous, sudden, and some call it their first instinct or initial intuition – that moment when something comes to you right before logic interrupts the thought or idea and attempts to dismiss the information you are receiving as irrational, untrue, imagined, or simply impossible. Those who are highly analytical or always thinking through things thoroughly or are "all in their head," or philosophical tend to demonstrate a strong ability when it comes to claircognizance.

Working with the Crown Chakra Exercise

As mentioned earlier, meditation is one of the primary tools you will use to deal with each of your psychic abilities and to trigger them into action. The same goes for the skills of clairsentience and claircognizance. This meditation will help you open up to the vibrations around you so that you can be a fine-tuned receiver of information when you choose to be.

You should commit to doing this exercise at least one a day and do so at the same time daily as it will train the brain to be ready for meditative work at the same time each day. Doing this exercise will help balance the Crown Chakra and keep it free from any blockage that might otherwise hinder your ability to receive incoming paraphysically-interpreted information.

Sit quietly and breathe in and out slowly. Focus on the breath until you are completely relaxed. Now focus on the top of your head where your

Crown Chakra is, and for about five minutes simply see it in your mind's eye, swirling around free of blockages and spinning in a rapid direction clockwise. The wheel spins with energetic colors of white, electric blue, and purple. Suddenly you watch as this rapid spinning energy vortex begins to transform into a lotus of 1000 petals and you get to witness its almost endless unfolding. Keep the image in your mind as long as your able. When you are finished just let the image fade away into the distance before you open your eyes and end the meditation session. Make sure you take notes on how you felt during the meditation, afterward, and note some of your experiences through the day if you suddenly notice you are more in tune with your feelings and thoughts on a physical level, but also on a paraphysical level.

Using Affirmations to Hone Your Abilities

Affirmations are powerful statements that help you establish a specific intention. If it is your intent to open your mind, free the Crown Chakra of blockages, and to improve upon any of your psychic abilities, affirmations can definitely serve you in this regard. The sentences or statements you use must be as brief and concise as possible: This makes them not only easy to remember but more meaningful to you. Some affirmations you might want to consider using include:

- *"I am open to the natural vibrations around me."* (or closed if you want to tone down your natural empathic abilities for a short period.)
- *"I am capable of feeling the emotions of others even without them conveying them to me in words or body language."*
- *"I am capable of clearly receiving the messages from my higher self."*
- *"I trust my intuition and psychic senses knowing they are available to me only for my highest good."*
- *"I trust the messages my higher self provides me with and act on the instructions accordingly."*

You can use any of the examples set forth here, but it is better to write your own so they are more meaningful to you. Once you have written a couple, put them on sticky notes and place them where you will see them and be reminded of them. Put them on the bathroom mirror, bedroom mirror, in your wallet, handbag, purse, backpack, glove box, desk drawer, on a bulletin board or simply use it as a bookmark so every time you pick up the book you are reminded to focus on the affirmation. You can say it aloud if you are alone or simply speak inside of your mind if you are in a crowded area or lack privacy. Use the affirmations daily as a reminder that you are attuned to your abilities and capable of trusting your Higher Self to serve as your guide. Remember to feel the affirmation emotionally and even use physical gestures (such as hands in the air) to connect to the affirmation more deeply.

Speak to the Divine

Asking the Divine for assistance when you are working with psychic abilities is certainly something that can prove beneficial, no matter what God or Divine Being you have an affinity with. Ask the Divine to keep any guidance or intuitive messages you receive as positive, and only for the higher good. A small prayer before beginning psychic work can definitely help in raising your vibrations as well so you can make yourself more receptive to energies and vibrations around you. Also, burning some incense can help you shift your state of mind from one grounded in the physical to one that is elevated and ready to pick up on higher energy vibrations. Frankincense or myrrh are recommended for psychic practices and endeavors, but nag champa and even dragon's blood incense are equally effective. This technique can be used with any of the psychic abilities you have and is a nice addition to the white light exercise to follows.

White Light Exercise

This exercise is perfect before you work with any of your paraphysical senses, but it is also great for times when you might feel overwhelmed or as if you have sensory overload – a common experience for those who are clairsentient and claircognizant. The exercise is simple, but truly effective.

Stand up straight and focus on a white light stemming from your solar plexus. Watch as this light grows larger and larger until it envelops you. Let this white light expand outward until it forms a bubble. When you are in this white light, no vibrations, or energies you do not want to experience can get in and you are not un-desirously drained from your energies either. The white light is a barrier, reflecting away excess energies and keeping in or retaining your own. The more you practice this exercise, the better you will get at keeping psychic attacks and episodes of psychic draining at bay. Bear in mind not all psychic attacks are intentional, but there are real life psychic vampires that can drain you of your energy. You've probably encountered a few in your lifetime where whenever you are around the person suddenly your good mood is gone, your energy dissipates dramatically, and you turn sullen, moody, and inward. You may even find you want to sleep. These things can happen quite unintentionally as well as some people who drain others of their energy on unaware they are doing so. At the same time, the white light bubble can block off others emotions so you don't become overwhelmed with too much sensory information all at once.

Clairolfactory & Clairgustance: Clear Scent and Taste

Clairolfactory, sometimes called clairessence, means true or clear smelling, and it is the detection of a scent with the paraphysical senses. One of the easiest methods for triggering your clairolfactory senses into action is to start using incense when meditating and to make use of essential oils, which are used for establishing specific moods and for natural healing purposes. By tuning into different scents you can hone your physical and paraphysical sense of clairessence. How do scents influence one's state of consciousness and how can they influence one to take on a higher state of consciousness so that different vibrations can be achieved? Think of it this way, the smell of something decaying will illicit and extremely different response from the smell of incense or an essential oil which is used for the purposes of cleansing the energies in a room and lifting one's conscious state to one of a higher vibration. Also, bear in mind that the physical sense of smell is uniquely tied to memory, so some paraphysical senses can trigger deep, hidden memories of the past, or you might have a clairvoyant or clairaudient experience accompany the clairessence, all of which serve to paint a picture of the past, present, or future. Some scents will work in helping you relax enough to tap into your skills as well: Consider the use of lavender to relax or the scent of orange essential oils to height your awareness.

Some scents detected through your psychic sense will be quite obvious. For example, if you are a non-smoker, the smell of smoke might offend you but prove easily recognizable. Some scents will prove very faint and fleeting, while others might overwhelm you. If you detect something, see if it reminds you of something in your own life in a symbolic sense. For instance, if the smell of cedar closet reminds you of your grandfather, then you smell cedar suddenly without a physical source nearby to provide the source of the scent, then the scent might indicate the presence of your grandfather's spirit, or the spirit of someone else's grandfather connecting with you through symbolism that you might be familiar with at the time.

Just as clairolfactory is the psychic sense of smell, clairgustance is the psychic sense of taste. With circumstance, you have probably guessed by now that you can taste something without any physical source for the taste. In a similar fashion, you might pick up on a taste that triggers a memory from your past or you might taste something entirely new to you that you are not sure of: For example, imagine picking up on the spirit of a person or even a person who is living and suddenly tasting chocolate only to later come to find out the individual was either a baker or worked with candy in some way. Of course, the symbolic language the High Self uses to connect with you and convey messages can serve up double entendres as well. Imagine picking up on someone's energies who leaves a sour taste in your mouth because they are bitter, or someone who leaves a sweet, warm taste in your mouth because they are by nature, friendly with a warm personality. Or, imagine tasting peanut butter or something nutty to convey that someone might not have all of their faculties about them.

Essentially, clairgustance is a means of experiencing the ethereal and spiritual worlds. The things one might taste will differ depending upon what one is connecting with and the reason for that connection. A person who is working with law enforcement might taste copper in the mouth, which is much like the taste of blood. Another might smell the scent of almonds, which is linked to cyanide. The tastes and scents detected might lead investigators to some clues on how to solve a particular case. Usually clairgustance experiences go hand-in-hand with clairolfactory experiences for reasons unknown, but it is most likely that you have to be able to smell some foods in order to taste them at all: Take cinnamon for example that has no taste whatsoever unless you can smell it while you are eating it.

Sweet & Sour Exercise

Make a deck or cards out of blank postcards or index cards. On each card depict a food item: noting its smell and taste. Once the deck is complete shuffle it. Turn the cards upside down so you cannot see what is on each card. Using one card at a time, see if you can taste or smell what is on the card. Note your successes and practice. See if you improve over the course of time.

Improving Awareness to Heighten Senses

Learning to heighten your awareness has the secondary benefit of allowing you to heighten your paraphysical senses. Simply doing this exercise every few days will definitely increase your awareness of your own body and your immediate surroundings.

Sit comfortably in a chair (don't lay down as you may become too relaxed and drift off to sleep, thereby defeating the purpose of the exercise.

Focus on your feet and see them as if you are seeing them for the first time (do this in your mind's eye). See the toes, their length, shape, the shape of the toe nails, the overall shape of your foot, the condition of the skin. Now sense how they feel. Are the cold, warm, in between? Are you wearing socks? Are they comfortable or too tight? What about shoes? How do they feel?

You will now begin to move up the body and do this with every stop you make. Sense your ankles, calves, knees, thighs, hips, pelvis, abdomen, chest, upper arms, elbows, lower arms, hands, fingers, shoulders, back, neck, and head. Scan each part of your body for muscular tension or pain. While you are doing so, if you encounter a painful or tense part of your body, ask your Higher Self why this part of the body is bothering you, then move on. The answers will eventually come to you as you practice.

Once you are done scanning your body, you will turn to scan the external environment. Can you sense what you are sitting on? What does it feel like against your body? What about the air in the room? Is it heavy or light against your skin? Is there a breeze? Is the air dry? Can you sense any emotion?

Practice this exercise on a regular basis to improve how you pay attention to your internal reactions and how you interact with the external environment. Tuning into the senses will also quiet the mind down and allow your own inner wisdom to slowly emerge.

Psychometry

Psychometry is the ability to pick up energy vibrations and information while holding onto an object. The information comes directly from the object in one's hand as it is believed that events can be imprinted on inanimate objects and later picked up on by our senses. Essentially, when this skill is honed, you should be able to pick up an inanimate object and tell something about that object, its owner, or some event or feeling it is connected with without knowing anything about the object beforehand. For instance, you might be able to describe the person who owns the piece, what they liked about it, why the piece was important to them, and the circumstances in which the obtained to object in the first place. It is believed by some that the atoms and molecules that come in constant contact with a person and the object mingle together and the object that becomes attached to part of the essence of that being and this is what those who perform psychometry pick up on when they detect energies from the object they hold. This is not such an unusual thought, as magickal practitioners often cleanse and charge objects with the specific duties that they carry out during magickal workings. Along the same lines, everyday objects can become charged with the energies of a person or environment.

When performing psychometry, the object is often placed in the left hand to receive information and in the right hand to be charged or blessed. Of course, the key here is the use of the dominant hand for charging and blessing, so if you are left handed, you will use your right hand to receive incoming information from psychometry sessions.

Opening Your Third Eye

Often when you are holding an object in your hands you will end up seeing images in your mind. Opening the third eye, located between the two brows just a bit above them, helps in getting clearer psychic images. Follow these steps to open the third eye while using psychometry:

1. Meditate before you try a psychometry session to heighten your awareness and vibration.
2. Light some incense to keep your awareness heightened during the psychometry session.
3. Hold the object in your dominant hand.

4. Silence your mind as much as you are able.
5. Allow images to appear to you and sense them in the location of your third eye.
6. Picture the eye opening up and being able to see with perfect clarity.
7. Let images which are fuzzy try to sharpen – don't question what you are seeing just remember.
8. Observe as long as you feel you are receiving more input or images.
9. Document what you've seen and compare your hits or misses.

Antiques and the Help of Others

Other means for practicing psychometry is through the use of antiques, old photo albums, and using a partner. With a partner, the person can bring small objects, jewelry, or other personal belongings of which they know the background. Then you can use your psychometry skills to read the said objects and your partner can let you know whether or not you are accurate with what you have sensed.

Summary

So, know you are familiar with the primary paraphysical senses you can use to experience the world in a whole new way. You will find that the paraphysical senses, once you work with them on a regular basis, will end up improving your interaction with the world, and your overall awareness of your surroundings, environment, and the people in your life. Even better, you will develop a relationship with your Higher Self and learn to trust your intuition as your guide. In doing, so you'll soon discover that your gut instincts are often dead on accurate and a tool that you can use for the betterment of your life as well as to help others. One final note: Don't be disappointed if you don't awaken or hone your psychic senses overnight. Remember that this will take work, but it is work that is well worth the effort! Keep practicing, and you will sharpen your skills in no time! Take Care of yourself.

Finally, if you did like my book I would really appreciate if you might be able to leave even just a small review on Amazon.

Thank you

Citations

8 Celebrities Who Had Premonitions That Came True: Philip Seymour Hoffman, Bam Margera. (2014, February 06). Retrieved March 19, 2017, from http://www.theepochtimes.com/n3/492335-celebrities-who-had-premonitions-that-came-true-philip-seymour-hoffman-whitney-houston-more/

Aberlin, M. B. (2016, September 01). **A Cornucopia of Sensory Perception**. Retrieved March 19, 2017, from http://www.the-scientist.com/?articles.view/articleNo/46782/title/A-Cornucopia-of-Sensory-Perception/

Clairvoyance. (n.d.). Retrieved March 19, 2017, from http://www.newworldencyclopedia.org/entry/Clairvoyance

ESP Is Put to the Test-Can You Foretell the Results? (2017, March 10).

Retrieved March 19, 2017, from http://news.nationalgeographic.com/news/2014/01/140121-esp-clairvoyance-sixth-sense-science-telepathy/

Lowery, B. (n.d.). A **Study showing that humans have some psychic powers caps Daryl Bem's career** | Cornell Chronicle. Retrieved March 19, 2017, from http://www.news.cornell.edu/stories/2010/12/study-looks-brains-ability-see-future

Online Etymology Dictionary. (n.d.). Retrieved March 19, 2017, from http://www.etymonline.com/index.php?term=psychic

Psychic Experience and the Brain with Vernon Neppe. (2016, May 02). Retrieved March 19, 2017, from https://www.youtube.com/watch?v=LGMiIE1b2L8

The Neuroscience of Psychic Experience. (n.d.). Retrieved March 19, 2017, from http://www.doctoroz.com/article/neuroscience-psychic-experience

The Wreck of the Titan: Or, Futility. (2017, March 16). Retrieved March 19, 2017, from https://en.wikipedia.org/wiki/The_Wreck_of_the_Titan:_Or,_Futility

What is Occam's Razor? (n.d.). Retrieved March 19, 2017, from http://math.ucr.edu/home/baez/physics/General/occam.html.

23843968R00038

Printed in Great Britain
by Amazon